The Unofficial Guide to Harry Potter® Collectibles

Kathy J. Wells

Schiffer® Publishing Ltd
4880 Lower Valley Road Atglen, Pennsylvania 19310

Disclaimer & Copyright

**Unless otherwise noted, images are the property of the author.*

Library of Congress Control Number: 2010941749

Designed by Stephanie Daugherty
Type set in LumosLatino/Lumos/Adobe Garamond Pro
ISBN: 978-0-7643-3673-7
Printed in China

Schiffer Publishing Ltd.
4880 Lower Valley Road
Atglen, PA 19310
Phone: (610) 593-1777; Fax: (610) 593-2002
E-mail: Info@schifferbooks.com

In Europe, Schiffer books are distributed by

Bushwood Books
6 Marksbury Ave.
Kew Gardens
Surrey TW9 4JF England
Phone: 44 (0) 20 8392 8585; Fax: 44 (0) 20 8392 9876
E-mail: info@bushwoodbooks.co.uk
Website: www.bushwoodbooks.co.uk

☆ ☆ ☆ ☆ ☆

Contents

Dedication

This book is for my wonderful and supportive family
Sabrina, Nathan, Megan, Kee, and Ty.

Acknowledgments

There are many people who helped put this guide together in such a short time. I am very grateful to my son, Nathan and his wife Megan for their support and encouragement. I would like to thank my forever friends, Mikki Marko and Barb Schneider.

Special thanks to numerous Harry Potter collectors, including Laura Crafts and Doug Potter, who took time from their busy schedules to share their personal collections and photographs with me. Thanks to Marjorie thorStraten, Amy Lowe, and BJ Washington for their encouragement and support.

This book would not be possible without the guidance of those at Schiffer Publishing. They made a new author's dream become a reality.

I would like to give special thanks to Michael Crawford, Gregory Crafts at Gentle Giant®, and Tom Courtney at Tonner®, who contributed photographs and information for this guide. Also, thank you to all the companies for granting their permissions to have their merchandise included here.

Finally, I would also like to thank J. K. Rowling for sharing her life with Harry Potter... May the magic never end!

Introduction

Where It All Began

The Harry Potter universe began when Harry Potter popped into J. K. Rowling's mind in 1990, while riding a train. After rejections from numerous publishers, Bloomsbury saw her vision and, in 1997, published *Harry Potter and the Philosopher's Stone*. Warner Bros. decided to release the first movie under two titles — "Philosopher's Stone" for the UK market and "Sorcerer's Stone" for the USA market. At that time, I was unaware of Harry's existence. Two years later, my world changed completely after reading the first three novels, *Harry Potter and the Sorcerer's Stone*, *Harry Potter and the Chamber of Secrets*, and *Harry Potter and the Prisoner of Azkaban*. I, like thousands of others, was hooked on Harry Potter!

My collection started with the purchase of Mattel's Professor Dumbledore action figure. Dumbledore's arm was assembled backwards.

Over time, my collection ballooned to include action figures, statutes, ornaments, stickers, calendars, and pretty much everything else.

I, like many others, wanted to know what mycollection was worth. Searching through the Internet, bookstores, and libraries for a Harry Potter price guide yielded next to nothing. There was only one partial guide and it was over ten years old. After due consideration, I decided to take the plunge and create this guide for all my fellow Harry Potter collectors.

This is not, however, an all-encompassing guide; not every action figure, toy, game, paper, or collectible is listed. Instead I have tried to focus on a limited selection of collectibles that I personally feel are at the forefront of today's collectible market.

Pricing

The prices listed are estimates and are not indicative of what the item should sell for. Prices vary by location, rarity, and economic conditions. What may sell for $100 today, may sell for $50 tomorrow, or visa-versa.

As any Harry Potter collector is aware, new items are being released every year and will continue to do so for the next couple of years in conjunction with the release of *Harry Potter and the Deathly Hallow*®, Parts I and II. Although products are released for the mass market, their value is not in short-term availability, but in the long-term sustainability. It may take as long as ten, fifteen, or twenty years for an action figure to become a rare collectible. For instance, the Mattel® series of toys released between 2001 and 2004 are beginning to reach their true potential. Collectors are just becoming aware that the Mattel figures are no longer being produced as NECA™ begins its release of Harry Potter products to the mass market. A Mattel action figure in its original packaging is highly collectible because most have been opened for play or display.

Time can also be the enemy of collectors. Finding an older version of an action figure in its original packaging in perfect condition is extremely rare. Time causes mishandling, which, in turn, causes fading, scratching, and tearing.

There are several companies that provide grading services for collectors who wish to sell their collectibles. Only the serious collector wishing for pristine packaging usually spends the extra dollars for these. The majority of collectors, myself included, are not as concerned about above mint condition. They want to have a complete series and a hobby grade is sufficient. The prices in this guide are for "hobby grade."

My research comes from numerous sources, including traditional online auction houses such as eBay, Yahoo, and Amazon. Prices were also researched through toy stores, other collectors, and from my own experience. However, I do not place a great emphasis on prices obtained through the auction houses since auctions are valued on the whims of a seller who may have many reasons for inflating or deflated pricing. Some just want to get rid of the item because they no longer want to store it, or they just need a little extra money, or they feel their items are worth a fortune. Buyers play the auction game, bidding up the price in a fever of bidding excitement, sometimes regretting it later. This is not the true value of a collectible. Sustainability in a moving market is the true value and you need to wait years for that.

In most instances, my research yielded positive results, yet there were some disappointments. You may, like I was, be delighted or disappointed at the various values listed in this guide. If you are disappointed, I would say to you, do not be discouraged — and do not throw away today what might be valuable tomorrow. Again, sustainability is the key.

I do not classify myself as a Harry Potter expert, but a Harry Potter collector. As such, the information in this guide is true to the best of my knowledge. If you come across any errors or just want give me your comments and hopefully encouragement, I would be more than happy to hear from you.

Photographs & Condition

Most all of the photographs in this guide are from my personal collection, taken by an amateur photographer — me. The rest of the photographs come from fellow collectors or companies.

Conditions range from mint, near mint, and poor. Mint condition is rare. It would be as if you picked it up from the manufacturer wearing cotton gloves. No bends or tears, crisp edges, absolutely no scratches in the blister pack (only a magnifying glass can find them).

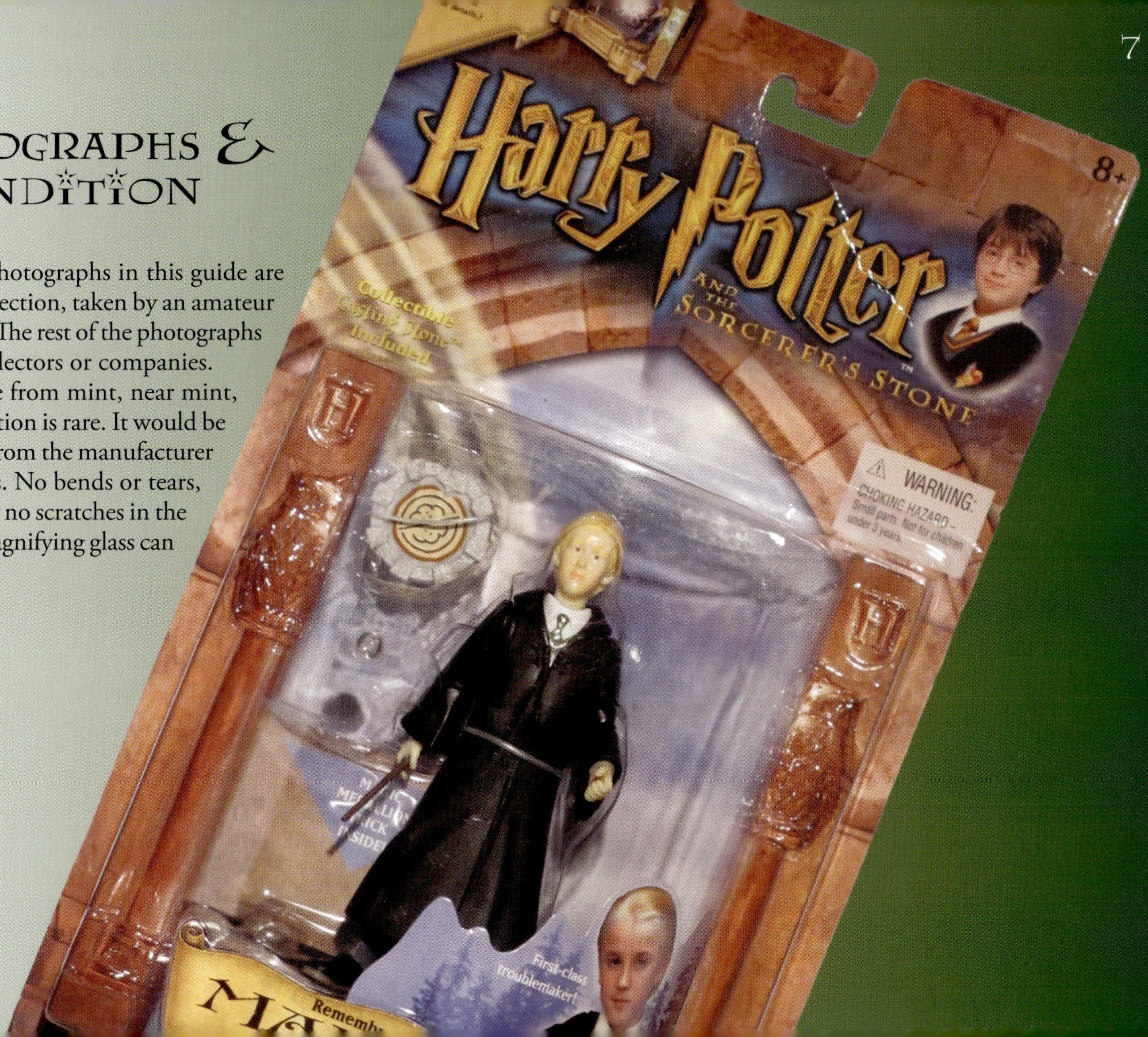

1

Harry Potter and the Sorcerer's Stone

Prior to Warner Bros. release of "Harry Potter and the Sorcerer's Stone" in November 2001, Mattel, Inc. won the much coveted master toy license from Warner Bros. Worldwide Consumer Products unit. Their initial concept was not to flood the market with products, but to roll them out in such a way to provide a long-term controlled product release.

The first action figures were released in October 2001 and came with a casting stone for use with the Electronic Powercasting Playset.

The Wizard Series

Gryffindor Harry, with Hedwig, in Hogwart's uniform without crest, ID 52664; *Value $60.* Rare with crest, *Value $100.*

Gryffindor Ron wearing Hogwart's uniform, rare with crest, ID 52665; *Value $100.*

Gryffindor Ron wearing Hogwart's uniform, without crest, ID 52665; *Value $60*

Schiffer Publishing
Your Source

Gryffindor Hermione wearing Hogwart's uniform, rare, ID 52670; *Value $100*

Slytherin Malfoy wearing Hogwart's uniform, rare with crest, ID 52668; *Value $95.*

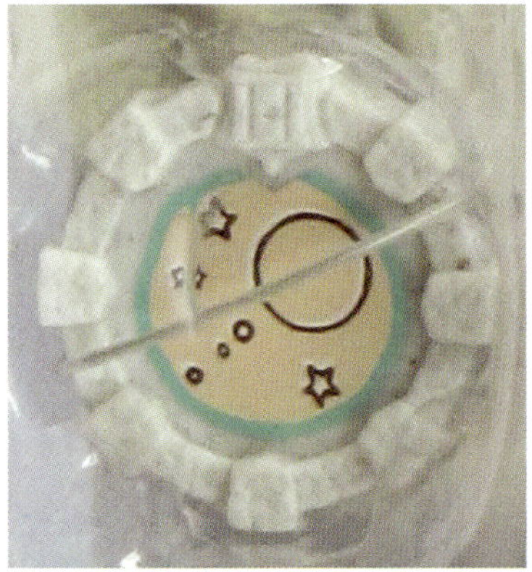

Slytherin Malfoy wearing Hogwart's uniform without crest, ID 52668; *Value $45.*

Remembrall Draco Malfoy, rare with crest, ID 52673, *Value $90*; without crest, *Value $45*.

Invisibility Cloak Harry, ID 52671; *Value $55.*

Professor Snape, ID 52666; *Value $45.*

Headmaster Dumbledore, very rare reverse arm, ID 52667; *Value $70-75.* With forward arm, *Value $40.*

Griphook, the Gringotts Goblin, with cart, ID 54879; *Value $35-40.*

Lord Voldemort with garlic necklace, ID 56096; *Value $30.*

Professor Quirrell, ID 52669; *Value $40.*

Lord Voldemort, Professor Quirrell with green face, no garlic necklace, ID 54877, rare, *Value $60.*

Hagrid, ID 52674; *Value $75.*

Magical Creatures

In addition to the Wizard action figures, in 2001 Mattel released a series of three Magical Creatures. It was a surprise to fans that Hagrid, the Hogwart's gamekeeper, was listed in this category. Fluffy *(value $50)* and the Mountain Troll *(value $65)* round out the trio.

Quidditch

Focusing on the Gryffindor House, Mattel ended the 2001 holiday season with Harry, Fred, and George. Fred is the rarest, with George following close behind. Harry is the easiest to find.T

Harry, with Snitch and black glasses, ID 56208; *Value $35.*

Fred, with beater's bat, extremely rare, ID 55530; *Value $100.*

George, with beater's bat, rare, ID 54875; *Value $85.*

Magical Scene Sets

In 2002, Mattel released Magical Mini's and Classic Scenes sets utilizing scenes from both the Sorcerer's Stone and Chamber of Secrets. Both sets are becoming increasingly harder to find, but finding the Classic Scenes in their original packaging is a real find.

In addition to Hagrid and Ginny, the Magical Mini's series also included:

- ☆ **Dumbledore** (with Fawkes), ID 474163, *Value $35*
- ☆ **Ron** (with Scabbers), ID 474132, *Value $33*
- ☆ **Hermione** in jeans, (with a Cat), ID 47414, *Value $50*
- ☆ **Hermione** in skirt, ID 474194, *Value $35*
- ☆ **Harry** in jeans, ID 474132, *Value $40*
- ☆ **Harry** (Quidditch), ID 474170, *Value $39*

Hagrid and Norbert, ID 47415; *Value $35.*

The Chamber of Keys, ID 50256; *Value $30.*

Ginny Weasley, ID 47419; *Value $35.*

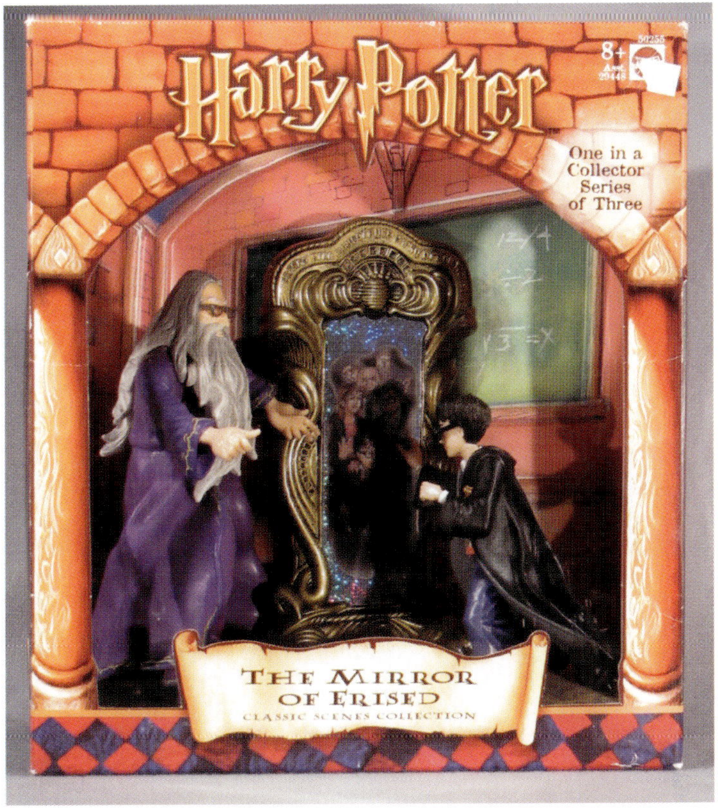

The Mirror of Erised, ID 50255; *Value $30.*

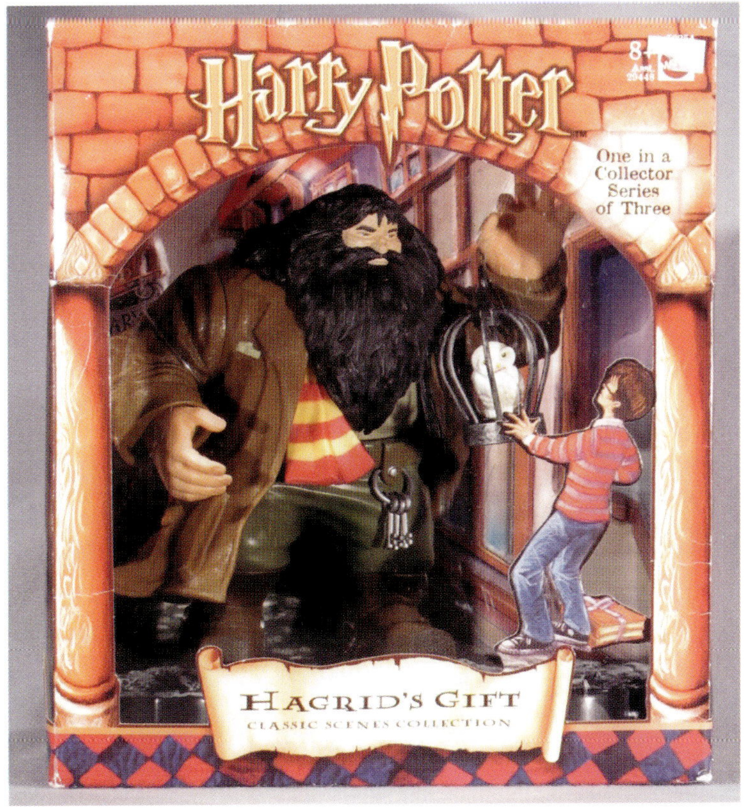

Hagrid's Gift, ID 0254; *Value $30.*

2

Harry Potter and the Chamber of Secrets

In anticipation of the release of "Harry Potter and the Chamber of Secrets" in 2002, Mattel released several series of action figures, adding to the Wizard and Magical Creatures collections.

Slime Chamber Series

The action figures in this series included a bottle of colored "slime" useful in potion-making with the Slime Chamber Playset. One figure pre-released under the Sorcerer's Stone Wizard series was Griphook the Goblin, whose packaging included a bottle of slime that could be used with this series.

Harry, wearing spiderweb robes, with blue slime, ID 54870; *Value $35.*

Author's Note: ***Draco Malfoy*** *is not featured here, but is valued at $50.*

Ron wearing slug robes, with red slime, ID 54871; *Value $50.*

Hermione with cat and pink slime, ID 54873; *Value $45.*

Fred, George, and purple slime. Although in separate packaging, both are identical, ID 54876. **Fred**, very rare, *Value $150;* **George,** *Value $90.*

The Seeker

Mattel added two new figures in the Chamber of Secrets series.

Seeker Harry Potter, flying cord guide, ID 56187; *Value $45.*

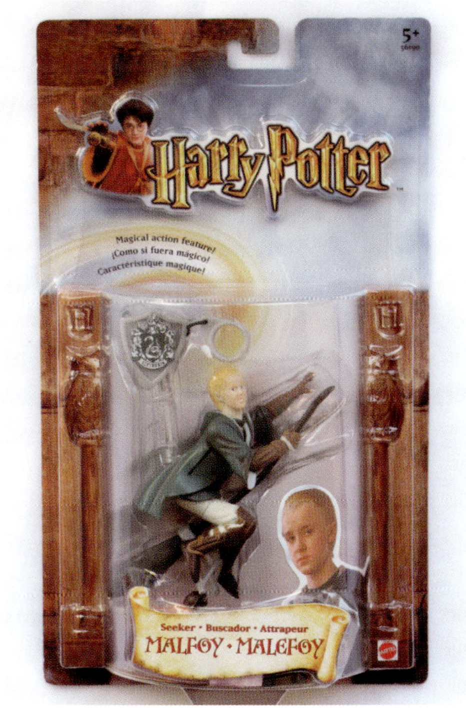

Seeker Draco Malfoy, flying cord guide, ID 56190; *Value $95.*

Wizard Series, Series II

*Author's Note: Action figures not featured here are **Professor Lockhart** with pixie cage valued at $30 and **Hermione Granger** valued at $90.*

Harry Potter with Sword, ID 56188; *Value $50.*

Professor Flitwick on stack of books, ID 56193; *Value $45.*

Professor Snape with cauldron, ID 56192; *Value $50.*

Dobby, the house elf, ID 56194; *Value $95.*

Cast – A – Spell and Dueling Club

Interactive dueling action figures enter the market.

Professor Lockhart, Dueling Club, ID 57602; *Value $29.*

Tom Riddle, Dueling Club, ID 56196;
Value $50.

Author's Note: Action figure not featured is ***Draco Malfoy****, ID 57604, value $95.*

Harry Potter, Cast-a-Spell, red arrow, ID 56189; *Value $35.*

Harry Potter, Dueling Club, ID 57601; *Value $20.*

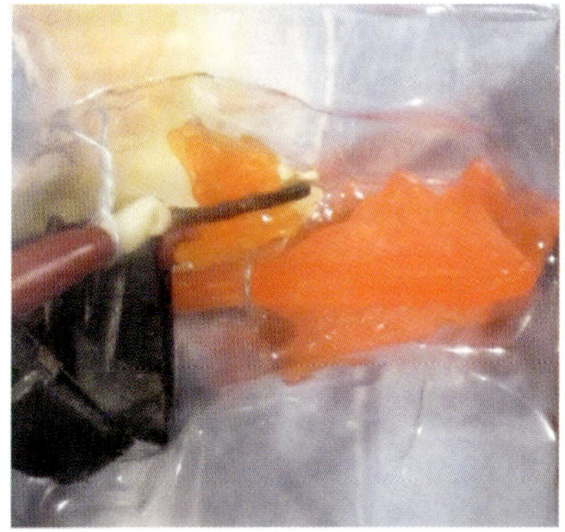

*Author's Note: Action figure not featured is **Ron Weasley**, ID 56191, value $65.*

Magical Creatures, Series II

As new creatures were introduced in "Harry Potter and the Chamber of Secrets," Mattel added four new creatures to its existing line:

- **Centaur,** ID 54882, Value $45
- **Norbert the Norwegian Ridgeback,** ID 55299, Value $55
- **Knight chess piece,** ID 55754, Value $35
- **Aragog,** ID 56628, Value $55

3

Harry Potter and the Prisoner of Azkaban

Mattel's last production under its license with Warner Bros. was to coincide with the release of "Harry Potter and the Prisoner of Azkaban." These were the first deviation in packaging with larger action figures geared more to the collector than as a toy.

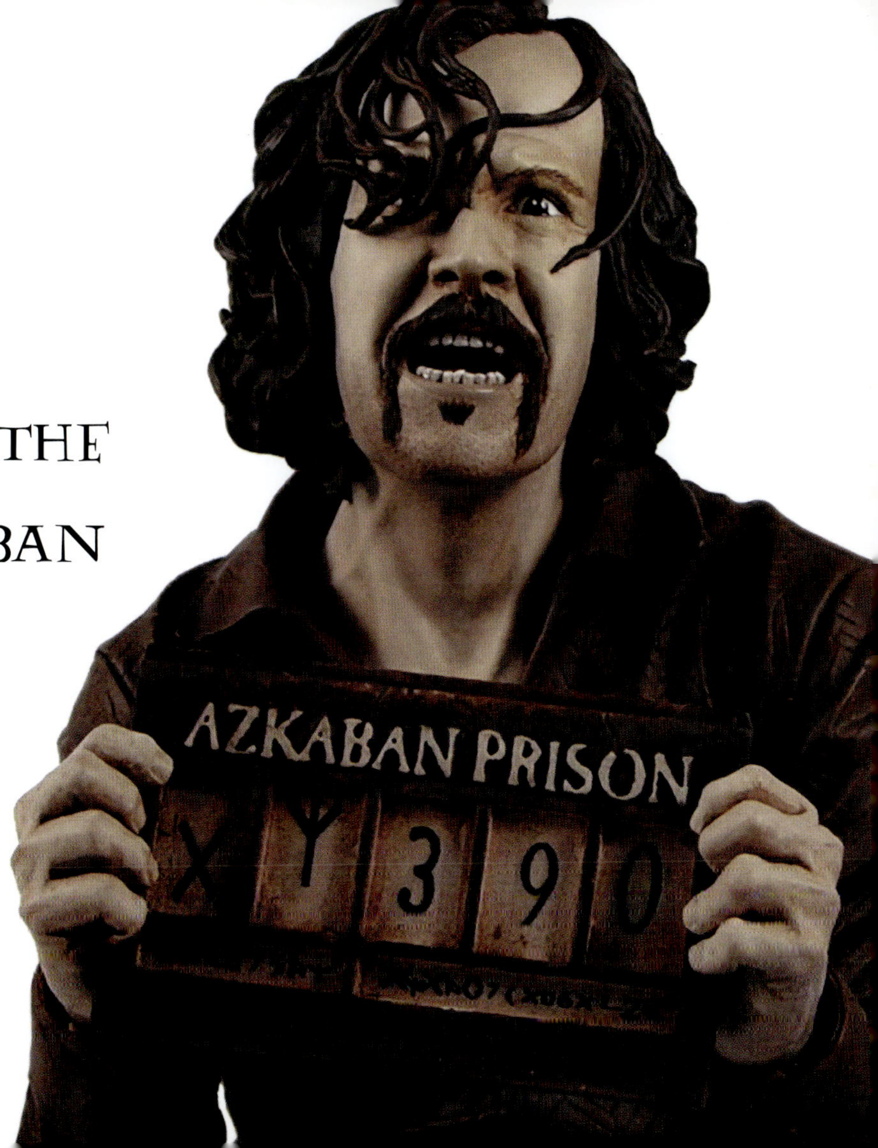

Magical Action Figures

A set of six Prisoner of Azkaban action figures were released, each having separate moving components.

Albus Dumbledore, ID C3151; *Value $55.*

Lord Voldemort, rare, ID C3152; *Value $95.*

Azkaban Dementor, ID C3159; *Value $55.*

Extreme Quidditch Harry, ID C3133; *Value $55.*
Courtesy of Michael Crawford.

Expecto Patronum Harry, ID C3145; *Value $55.*

Professor/Werewolf Lupin, ID C3147; *Value $65.*

Box Sets

These mini-box sets were the last products released by Mattel, as the company, for various economic reasons, decided to end their Warner Bros. Harry Potter license.

Harry, Malfoy, Buckbeak—
Series 1, ID C3154; *Value $35.*

Harry, Dementor, Sirius, Werewolf
Series 1, ID C3155; *Value $35.*

Harry, Lupin, Werewolf—
Series 1, ID C3156; *Value $35.*

Harry, Hermione, Ron (in Hogwart's Uniform)—Series 1, ID C3157; *Value $35.*

Harry, Hermione, Ron (in street clothes)—
Series 2, ID C3160; *Value $35.*

Harry, Malfoy, Weasley twin, (Quidditch) Series 2, ID C3163; *Value $35.*

Harry, Snape, Dumbledore—
Series 2, ID C3162; *Value $35.*

4

Harry Potter and the Goblet of Fire

The next and current licensee for the Warner Bros. toy line is NECA™ or the National Entertainment and Collectibles Association™. Unfortunately, Harry Potter collectors had to wait three years between product releases. Finally, in February 2007, NECA previewed its first release of "Harry Potter and the Goblet of Fire" action figures and accessories at the annual New York toy trade show. NECA's marketing division realized that Harry Potter fans have aged since the release of Mattel products in 2001, and their products were now geared to adult collectors as well as young adults.

NECA

NECA's production department rolled out the action figures in assorted case quantities. Because of this, there is an overabundance of some actions figures and very limited quantities of others, which affects the value tremendously. As with most collectibles, the action figures that were released in limited quantities have retained or gained in value. NECA has strategically halted production on some of the action figures, which should cause a future increase in their value.

Series 1

NECA released only one series relating to "Harry Potter and the Goblet of Fire."

Tri-Wizard Champion Harry Potter, ID 49101; *Value $25.*

Lord Voldemort, ID 49105; *Value $60.*

Death Eater (Skull), ID 49103; *Value $27.*

Death Eater (Mask), ID 49102; *Value $27.*

Dementor, ID 49104; *Value $70.*

Death Eater (Skull), ID 49103; *Value $27.*

Death Eater (Mask), ID 49102; *Value $27.*

5

Harry Potter and the Order of the Phoenix

After the success of their first release in 2007, NECA was more ambitious with "Harry Potter and the Order of the Phoenix," releasing several series.

Series 1: The Build-up

Series 1 began with action figure packaging including a bogart/ dementor build-up. NECA has retired this series. The value on a complete set of four would be $275.

Action figures, set of four, 3.75", without build-up; *Value $40.*

Harry Potter in grey jumper, with bogart build-up, ID 60008. Retired in 2010; *Value $25.*

Ronald Weasley, with bogart build-up, ID 60023. Retired in 2010; *Value $60.*

Hermione Granger, with bogart build-up, Rare, ID 60015. Retired 2010; *Value $75.*

Sirius Black, with bogart build-up, ID 60030. Retired in 2010; *Value $40.*

Series 2

Professor Dumbledore, ID 60536; *Value $55.*

Death Eater with green mask, ID 60537.
Value with packaging error (title upside down), $65; correct version, $35.

Harry Potter, in Gryffindor Cardigan, ID 60535; *Value $20.*
SDCC, with Owl, *Value $30.*

Professor Severus Snape, ID 60539; *Value $60.*

Death Eater, silver mask, ID 60538; *Value $35.*

Series 3

Bellatrix Lestrange, ID 49157.
Retired in 2010, *Value $35.*

Lucius Malfoy, with Death Eater mask and cane, ID 49156. Retired in 2010, *Value $35.*

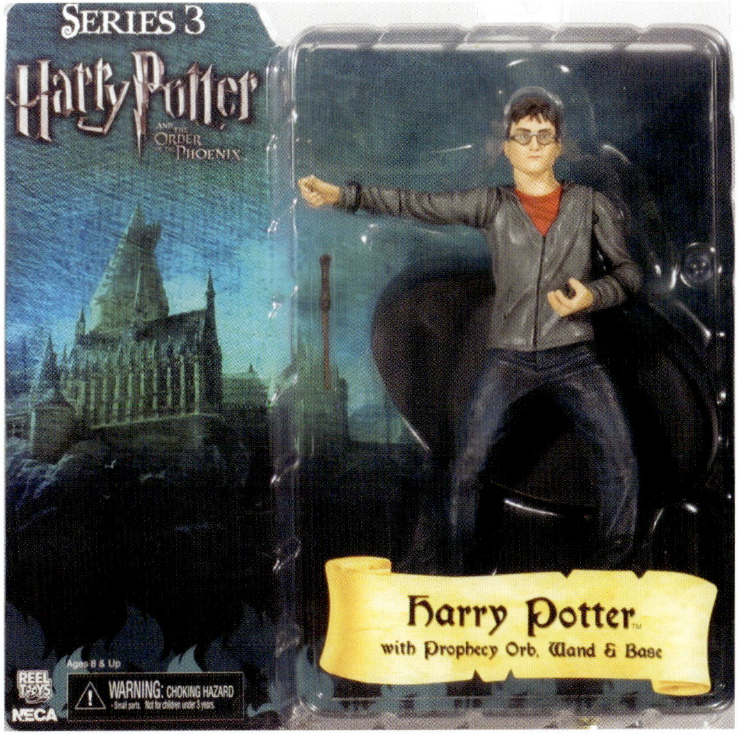

Harry Potter, in grey sweater, holding prophecy, ID 49155. Retired in 2010, *Value $28.*

Larger Action Figures

NECA's next marketing campaign was to introduce larger action figures to the collectible market, with an added twist — sound. These action figures spoke memorable quotes from the movie "Harry Potter and the Order of the Phoenix."

Harry Potter with sound;
12" — ID 49106, *Value $30;*
18" — ID 49107, *Value $40.*

Ron Weasley, 12" figure with sound, ID 60524; *Value $35.*

Hermione Granger, 12" figure with sound, ID 60523; *Value $40.*

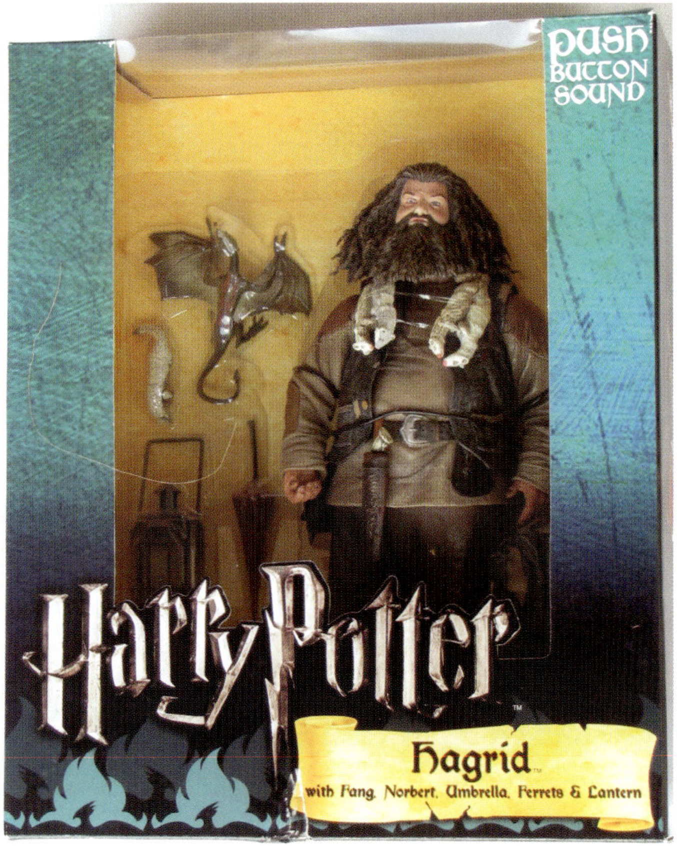

Deluxe Hagrid Figure with sound, 9.75". It includes light-up lamp, **Fang, and Norbert**, ID 60013; *Value $45. Photos courtesy of Michael Crawford,*

Diorama

NECA released a set of four dioramas in conjunction with "Harry Potter and the Order of the Phoenix."

However, the Professor Snape and Hermione diorama boxes were poorly designed, resulting in an extreme amount of damage to these two figures. NECA halted production for a limited time to fix the problem out of China. Unfortunately, packaging is still a problem and damage continues. If you can find a Snape or Hermione in perfect condition, expect to pay a premium price, especially for Snape.

Severus Snape, ID 60563; *Value $100.*

Harry Potter, ID 60562; *Value $30.*

Ron Weasley, ID 60565; *Value $35.*

Hermione Granger, ID 60564; *Value $65.*

Box Sets

Harry vs. Voldemort in graveyard, ID 60448; *Value, $40.*

Harry, Richard Harris as Dumbledore, with Fawkes the phoenix, ID 60561; *Value $65.*

6

Harry Potter and the Half Blood Prince

This series of action figures were introduced in 2009 just before the movie release of "Harry Potter and the Half Blood Prince."

In addition to the single packaging, NECA created two promotional limited release box sets. Their companion line of 3.75" figures swapped Voldemort for Mad-Eye Moody. Consequently, the 3.75" Voldemort is much in demand.

Author's Note: I have noticed a significant decrease in action figure production as the movies are winding down to their conclusion. Wise collectors will add to their collections early when the figures are released and hang on to them. NECA has begun to discontinue several earlier lines, which should see a significant increase in value.

Draco Malfoy, ID 60572; *Value $17.*

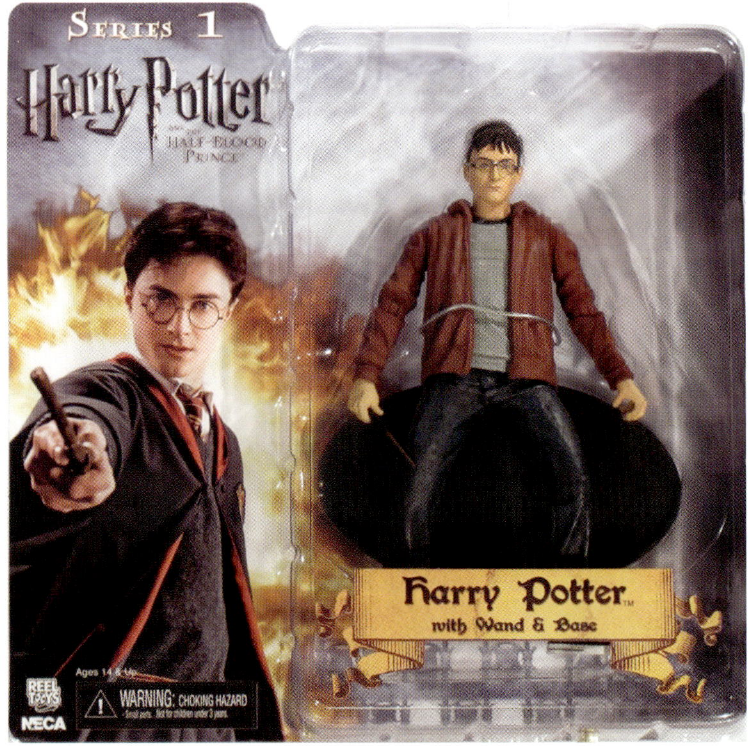

Harry Potter, ID 60573; *Value $25.*

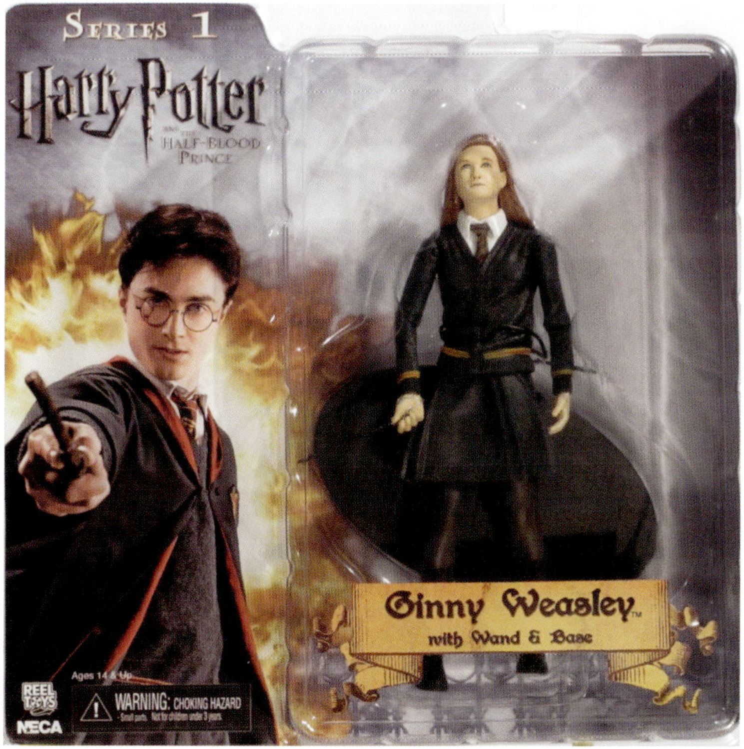

Ginny Weasley, ID 60570; *Value $25.*

Mad-Eye Moody, ID 60587; *Value $20.*

Draco Malfoy and Mad-Eye Moody Box Set, ID 59579; *Value $30.*

Harry Potter and Ginny Weasley Box Set, ID 59580; *Value $35.*

Action figures, 3.75", four-piece set; *Value $60.*

3.75" **Voldemort,** *Value $28.*

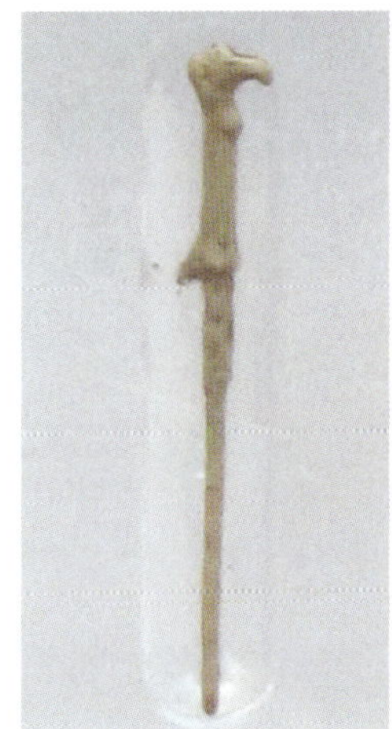

7

Harry Potter Busts and Statues

Gentle Giant Studios, Inc. is the parent company of Gentle Giant, Ltd., "the leading provider of both digital and physical three-dimensional models for the entertainment and consumer goods industries. Utilizing state-of-the-art digital technology combined with traditional sculpting techniques, Gentle Giant assures accuracy and quality in model design, creation, and prototyping."

Gentle Giant has taken the lead in Harry Potter collectibles with its line of mini-busts, bust-ups, and statuettes. Each has been issued in limited editions. The early releases (2007) are commanding exceptional prices. When collecting Gentle Giant, the older the release the more valuable it becomes, so grab these early and hang on to them.

GENTLE GIANT

STUDIOS

Mini-busts

Gentle Giant, Ltd. continued with mini versions of some favorite characters by creating mini bust-ups

Harry Potter, released 10/2005, ID 7396, LE 2000; *Value $155.*
Photo courtesy of Gentle Giant, Ltd.

Professor Dumbledore (Gambone),
released December 2005, ID 7590, LE 1500; *Value $75.*
Photo courtesy of Gentle Giant, Ltd.

Harry Potter/Year 5, released June 2007, ID 8792, LE 5000; *Value $50.* SDCC Special Edition/Light up, released June 2007, ID 8792LU; *Value $80.*

Sirius Black, Wanted Poster, released 10/2005, ID 7564, LE 1500; *Value $125.* *Photo courtesy of Gentle Giant, Ltd.*

Sirius Black, Wanted, SDCC Exclusive, ID 8157, LE 500, released July 2005; *Value $175.* *Photo courtesy of Gentle Giant, Ltd.*

Draco Malfoy, released June 2007, ID 9779, LE 2500*; Value $38.*

Richard Harris as **Dumbledore,** released July 2009, ID 12163, LE 750; *Value $110.*

Lord Voldemort, released April 2007, ID 9241, LE 2500; *Value $95.*

Fred and George Weasley, released April 2008, ID 10624, LE 2000; *Value $90. Photo courtesy of Michael Crawford.*

Professor Severus Snape,
released December 2005,
ID 7565, LE 1500;
Value $318.

Professor McGonagall,
released Junc 2008,
ID 10603, LE 1400;
Value $80.Photo courtesy of Gentle Giant, Ltd.

Remus Lupin, general public, released June 2008, ID 10600, LE 1250; *Value $55.* *Photo courtesy of Gentle Giant, Ltd.*

Remus Lupin, open mouth – SDCC, released August 2008, ID 11079, LE 500; *Value $110.*

Cho Chang, released June 2007, ID 9778, LE 2500; *Value $37.*

Ronald Weasley in Quidditch Gear, released January 2009, ID 11604A, LE 700; *Value $60.*

Harry Potter in Quidditch Gear, released August 2009, ID 11387, LE 850; *Value $55.*

OOTP **Sirius Black,** ID 10622, LE 800, released 2010; *Value $100. Courtesy of Gentle Giant, Ltd.*

Kreacher Mini Bust, ID 10605, LE 600, released 2010; *Value $80. Courtesy of Gentle Giant, Ltd.*

Fenrir Greyback, ID 11390, LE 600, released 2010; *Value $65. Courtesy of Gentle Giant, Ltd.*

Cedric Diggory, ID 80041, LE 750, released 2010; *Value $99. Courtesy of Gentle Giant, Ltd.*

Bellatrix Lestrange, released April 2008, ID 10599, LE 2500; Value $75. *Photo courtesy of Gentle Giant, Ltd.*

Death Eater, released August 2006, ID 8690, LE 1500; *Value $75.*

Nymphadora Tonks, released February 2008, ID 10546, LE 2500; *Value $45. Courtesy of Gentle Giant, Ltd.*

Hermione,
released November 2006,
ID 7633, LE 2500;
Value $75.

Dobby the House Elf, released April 2006,
ID 7645, LE 2000; *Value $100.*

Dementor, released April 2006, ID 8396, LE 1500; *Value $95. Courtesy of Gentle Giant, Ltd.*

Ron Weasley Yule Ball, released November 2006, ID 7632, LE 2000; *Value $50.*

Nearly Headless Nick, released August 2006, ID 7631, LE 1500; *Value $40.*
Courtesy of Gentle Giant, Ltd.

Ginny Weasley, released April 2009, ID 11605, LE 700; *Value $140.*

Mad Eye Moody, released March 2007, ID 9486, LE 1750; *Value $65.*

Luna Lovegood,
SDCC exclusive,
released July 2007,
ID HOL10224; *Value $142.*

Rebeus Hagrid,
released March 2007,
ID 7652, LE 2000;
Value $75.

Riddle Grave,
released April 2007,
ID 9144, LE 1500; *Value $55.*

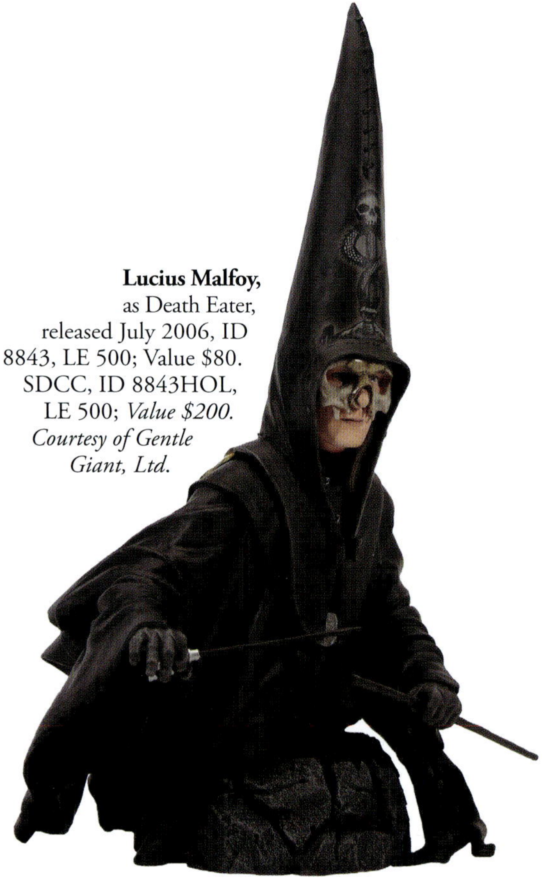

Lucius Malfoy, as Death Eater, released July 2006, ID 8843, LE 500; Value $80. SDCC, ID 8843HOL, LE 500; *Value $200. Courtesy of Gentle Giant, Ltd.*

Harry Potter OOTP includes **Harry Potter, Draco Malfoy, Professor Dumbledore, Neville Longbottom, Ginny Weasley,** ID: 9791-1 to 9791-5; *Value $35 for set of 5. Photos courtesy of Gentle Giant, Ltd.*

Harry Potter Classic Moments includes **Gryffindor Harry Potter, Ron Weasley, Hermione Granger, Tri-Wizard Harry Potter, Lord Voldemort,** ID: 9790-1 to 9790-5; *Value $35 for set of 5. Courtesy of Gentle Giant, Ltd.*

Statues

Gentle Giant, Ltd. decided to release a very small number of Harry Potter statues. The most impressive of these is the Hungarian Horntail. The attention to detail is superlative.

The Hungarian Horntail will garner much more attention with the opening of the ride at Universal's Wizarding World of Harry Potter™. The first edition releases will command higher prices.

Hungarian Horntail,
ID 8069, LE 1500;
Value $300.

Harry Potter on Thestral Statue, ID 10645, LE 1750; *Value $125.*

Merperson and Grindylow,
ID 8198, LE 500; *Value $150.*

8

Harry Potter Dolls

"The Tonner Doll Company is internationally renowned for award-winning dolls that encourage the young — and the young-at-heart — to Believe in the Power of Play®. Inspired by a passion for doll collecting, the company has manufactured fine dolls designed and sculpted by Robert Tonner, from little girl and classic character dolls that recapture the magic of childhood memories, to fully articulated high fashion dolls with exquisite collections of costumes that depict the quintessential American style. Robert Tonner's life-long interest in dolls, top-level fashion designer experience, and designing and sculpting talents led to his creation of the Tonner Doll Company, one of the most successful and celebrated doll manufacturers in the world."

The Tonner Harry Potter doll collection began with the first release of Harry, Hermione, and Ron at the 2007 New York toy trade show. They have consistently added new pieces every year. All dolls are issued under limited edition quantities and new releases command the best prices. Older releases are experiencing a decrease in value, but, once again, sustainability is the key in the long-term market.

TONNER®

Author's Note: Tonner dolls are created for young and old alike, but are not for those under 14 years of age. All images are courtesy of Tonner Doll Company, Inc. Photography by Storm Photo, Inc., Kingston, NY © Tonner Doll Company, Inc., all rights reserved.

Harry Potter at Yule Ball, LE 2500, ID T5-HPDD-01; *Value $120. Courtesy Tonner Doll Company, Inc.*

Harry Potter at Hogwarts, LE 5000, ID T5-HPDD-02; *Value $112. Courtesy Tonner Doll Company, Inc.*

Harry Potter as the Gryffindor Seeker, LE 2500, ID T6-HPDD-06; *Value $130. Courtesy Tonner Doll Company, Inc.*

Harry Potter is out of the classroom, LE 1000, ID T6-HPOF-01; *Value $80. Courtesy Tonner Doll Company, Inc.*

Harry – FAO – with trunk, *Value $399. Courtesy Tonner Doll Company, Inc.*

Ronald Weasley at Hogwarts, LE 5000, ID T6-HPDD 01; *Value $112. Courtesy Tonner Doll Company, Inc.*

Ronald Weasley at Yule Ball, LE 5000, ID T6-HPDD-03; *Value $249. Courtesy Tonner Doll Company, Inc.*

Ronald Weasley in casual clothes, LE 1000, ID T6-HPOF-03; *Value $75. Courtesy Tonner Doll Company, Inc.*

Hermione Granger at Hogwarts, LE 5000, ID T6-HPDD-02; *Value $169. Courtesy Tonner Doll Company, Inc.*

Hermione Granger at Yule Ball, LE 2500, ID T6-HPDD-04; *Value $150. Courtesy Tonner Doll Company, Inc.*

Hermione Granger is out of the classroom, IDT6-HPOF-04; *Value $120. Courtesy Tonner Doll Company, Inc.*

Professor Dumbledore (Richard Harris), LE 500, ID T9HPDD01; *Value $212. Courtesy Tonner Doll Company, Inc.*

Bellatrix Lestrange, LE 1000, ID T9HPDD01, released 2009; Value $175. *Courtesy Tonner Doll Company, Inc.*

Professor Severus Snape, LE 1500, ID T8-HPDD-02; *Value $225. Courtesy of Tonner Doll Company, Inc.*

Lord Voldemort,
ID 7HP0005, LE 1500; *Value $100.*
Courtesy Tonner Doll Company, Inc.

Lord Voldemort
FAO, LE 500; *Value $150.*
Courtesy of Tonner Doll Company, Inc.,

Lucius Malfoy, Death Eater,
LE 1000, ID T9HPDD03; *Value $215.*
Courtesy of Tonner Doll Company, Inc.

Kreacher House Elf,
ID T8-HPDD-03; *Value $90.*
Courtesy of Tonner Doll Company, Inc

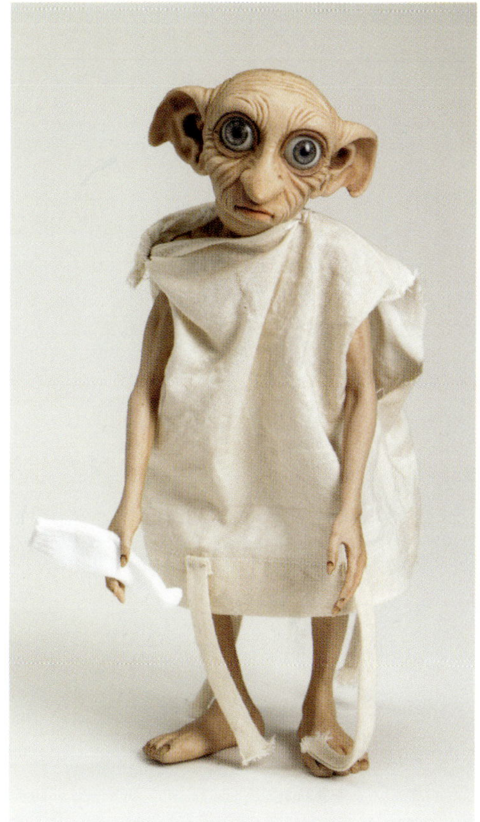

Dobby the House Elf,
ID T7-HPDD-04; *Value $90.*
Courtesy of Tonner Doll Company, Inc.

Draco Malfoy (Quidditch)
SDCC; *Value: $130.*
Courtesy Tonner Doll Company, Inc.

Draco Malfoy at Hogwarts, LE 5000,
ID T7-HPDD-04; *Value $112.*
Courtesy Tonner Doll Company, Inc.

Draco Malfoy FAO,
LE 200; *Value $150.*
Courtesy Tonner Doll Company, Inc.

Ginny Weasley at Hogwarts,
LE 1000, ID T9HPDD04; *Value $160.*
Courtesy Tonner Doll Company, Inc.

Luna Lovegood at Hogwarts,
LE 2000, ID T8-HPDD-04; *Value $160.*
Courtesy of Tonner Doll Company, Inc.

Cho Chang Yule Ball FAO; *Value $160.*
Courtesy of Tonner Doll Company, Inc.

Cho Chang at Hogwarts,
LE 2500, ID T8-HPDD-01; *bValue $142.*
Courtesy of Tonner Doll Company, Inc.

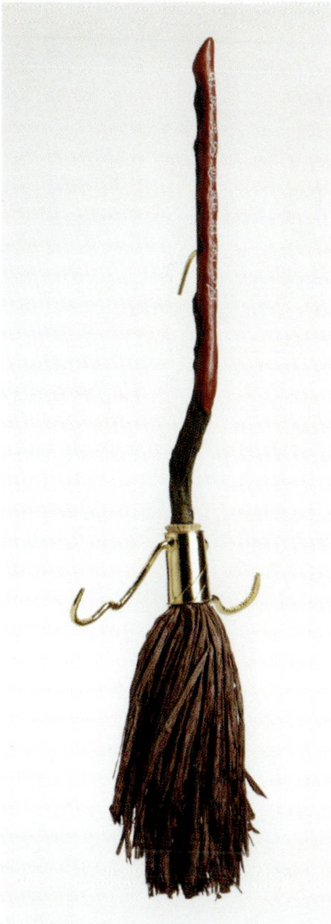

Firebolt, ID T6-HPAC-02; *Value $50. Courtesy of Tonner Doll Company, Inc.*

Hedwig Owl, ID T6-HPAC-01; *Value $50. Courtesy of Tonner Doll Company, Inc.*

Fawkes Phoenix, ID T7-HPAC-07; *Value $68. Courtesy of Tonner Doll Company, Inc.*

Tonner also created a line of accessories to accompany their Harry Potter dolls. These were not released in limited edition quantities and are still available. The Quidditch trunk is the hardest to find and its value has seen an increase over the past months.

Crookshanks Cat, ID T6-HPAC-05; *Value $30. Courtesy of Tonner Doll Company, Inc.*

Sorting Hat,
ID T7-HPAC-06; *Value $40.*
Courtesy of Tonner Doll Company, Inc.

Tri-Wizard Cup,
ID T6-HPAC-04; *Value $40.*

Quidditch Accessories, ID T6-HPAC-06; *Value $95.*
Courtesy of Tonner Doll Company, Inc.

Bibliography & Resources

In addition to the following sources, the reverse side of the packing is the most informative relating to which action figures belong with individual series. I have included photographs of the reverse packaging for reference.

Gentle Giant Studios,
accessed January 29, 2010; www.gentlegiantltd.com/help/studio.

Tonner Doll Company, Inc.,
accessed January 29, 2010; www.tonnerdoll.com/abouttonner.html.

Checklists, FigureRealm.com,
accessed January 30, 2010; www.figurerealm.com.

The Leaky Cauldron,
accessed February 18, 2010; www.the-leaky-cauldron.org.

General Info, Mugglenet's Harry Potter Timeline, Mugglenet.com,
accessed February 18, 2010; mugglenet.com.

Harry Potter and the Sorcerer's Stone
Includes:
• Poseable figure
• Magic wand
• Scabbers™
• Magic medallion trick
The day Harry Potter™ entered Hogwarts™ School of Witchcraft and Wizardry, his life changed forever. He never even knew he was a famous wizard and now, through a magical twist of fate, he's at an extraordinary place he never dreamed existed.
Join Harry and his friends on their magical adventures.
Ron Weasley™ has a lot to live up to. He is the sixth Weasley brother to attend Hogwarts™ and this year, his older brother Percy is a Prefect for Gryffindor™. To make things worse, Ron is stuck bringing the family pet, Scabbers the rat, to school with him. Thankfully his new best friend, Harry Potter™ is there to make things a lot more exciting!
Collectible Casting Stone™
Magic Medallion Trick Inside!
Make Magic Adventures Happen!
Collect them all!
Deluxe Creature Collection
Wizard Collection
Limited Quantity Available
PROOF OF PURCHASE
For information on Harry Potter visit www.harrypotter.com.
Harry Potter
Hermione
Slime Chamber™ Series
Includes:
• Poseable figure
• Potion bottle
• Cauldron with lid
• Orange SLIME™ compound
According to Moste Potente Potions, Polyjuice Potion will transform you into somebody else. When Hermione Granger™ brews this complicated potion, she adds one wrong ingredient so instead of turning into Millicent Bulstrode, she changes into Millicent's cat!
SLIME-OOZING FUN!
Drop SLIME™ compound on the Slime Chamber™ Series figures!
Make Magic Adventures Happen!
Collect them all!
QUIDDITCH™ TEAM
SLIME CHAMBER™ SERIES
Includes colored SLIME™ compound!
SLIME CHAMBER™ Playset
You control the slime-oozing snake!
WIZARD COLLECTION
Each sold separately, subject to availability. Colors and decorations may vary.
PROOF OF PURCHASE
SAFETY TESTED.
For more information on Harry Potter™ visit www.harrypotter.com.
For more information on Mattel Harry Potter™ products visit www.mattel.com/harrypotter

II
Harry Potter™
GINNY WEASLEY™
• MAGICAL MINIS™
• COLLECTION • COLECCION
ADVERTENCIA:
PUEDE CAUSAR ASFIXIA.
No recomendable para menores de 3 años. Contiene piezas pequeñas. 3+
47419
47417
47418
• POSEABLE • ARTICULADA • ARTICULÉE
• COLLECT THEM ALL! • ¡COLECCIÓNALOS! • COLLECTIONNE-LES TOUTES!
• Each sold separately, subject to availability. Colours and decorations may vary.
• Se venden por separado y están sujetos a disponibilidad. Los colores y decoración del producto pueden ser distintos de los mostrados.
• Tous vendus séparément. Certains produits peuvent ne pas être commercialisés. Les couleurs et les décorations peuvent varier.
U.S.A. CONSUMER INFORMATION
INFORMACIÓN PARA EL CONSUMIDOR EN LOS E.U.A.
CANADIAN CONSUMER INFORMATION
SERVICE À LA CLIENTÈLE CANADIENNE
CONFORMS TO THE SAFETY REQUIREMENTS OF ASTM F963. CONFORME AUX NORMES DE SÉCURITÉ. CUMPLE CON TODAS LAS NORMAS DE SEGURIDAD.
0 74299 47419 4
HARRY POTTER, characters, names and all related indicia are trademarks of and © Warner Bros.
WB SHIELD: ™ & © 2001 Warner Bros.
Used under license.
(S02)
HARRY POTTER, les personnages, les noms et tous les indices qui y sont associés sont des marques de Warner Bros.
ÉCUSSON WB : ™ & © 2001 Warner Bros.
Utilisation sous licence.
(S02)
47419
Ass. 47404
MATTEL

More fun with Harry Potter™ playsets! Collect them all!
¡Más diversión con conjuntos de juego de Harry Potter™! ¡Colecciónalos todos!
Ajoute au plaisir avec les coffrets Harry Potter™! Collectionne-les tous!
Harry
Dementor™
Sirius Black™
C3165
C3166
C3154
C3156
C3157
Contents: 3 Figures, 1 accessory. • Contenido: 3 figuras y accesorio. • Contient : 3 figurines et 1 accessoire.
www.harrypotter.com
SAFETY - TESTED. CONFORMS TO ASTM F963.
CONFORME AUX NORMES DE SÉCURITÉ. CUMPLE CON TODAS LAS NORMAS DE SEGURIDAD.
C3155
www.mattel.com
MATTEL
0 27084 10450 9

1 Articulated figure • Figura articulada
Figurine articulée
2 Launching spell • Hechizo lanzable
Sortilège à lancer
3 Detailed sculpting • Escultura detallada
Sculpture détaillée
4 Spell blast accessory/display stand
Accesorio lanza-hechizo/base de muestra
Accessoire jeteur de sortilège / socle
Display.
Muestra.
Montre-le.
Launch.
Lanza. • Propulse-le.
Reset.
Restablece. • Réenclenche-le.
Attach.
Conecta. • Fixe-le.
LEGENDS • LEYENDAS
Collect them all! • ¡Colecciónalos todos! • Collectionne-les toutes!
DELUXE
DE LUJO
CONTENTS: Figure, 2 accessories.
CONTENIDO: Figura y accesorios.
CONTIENT : Figurine et 2 accessoires.
MADE IN CHINA. Manufactured for Mattel.

Harry Potter
SERIES 1
Harry Potter
Harry Potter
Lord Voldemort
Dementor
Death Eater
Death Eater
TM & © Warner Bros. Entertainment Inc.
Harry Potter Publishing Rights © JKR
(s07)
AOL Keyword: HARRY POTTER
www.harrypotter.com
For more information on this specific
product, visit www.necaonline.com
NECA
MADE IN CHINA

Harry Potter
and the Order of the Phoenix
Series 1
Harry Potter
Hermione Granger
Ron Weasley
Sirius Black
Hermione Granger
TM & © Warner Bros. Entertainment Inc.
Harry Potter Publishing Rights © JKR
(s07)
AOL Keyword: HARRY POTTER
www.harrypotter.com
For more information on this specific
product, visit www.necaonline.com
NECA c/o Francis Melinek
Star Images
35 D Newington Green
London N16 9PR
UNITED KINGDOM
Telephone: 44+2072494662
0-3
MADE IN CHINA

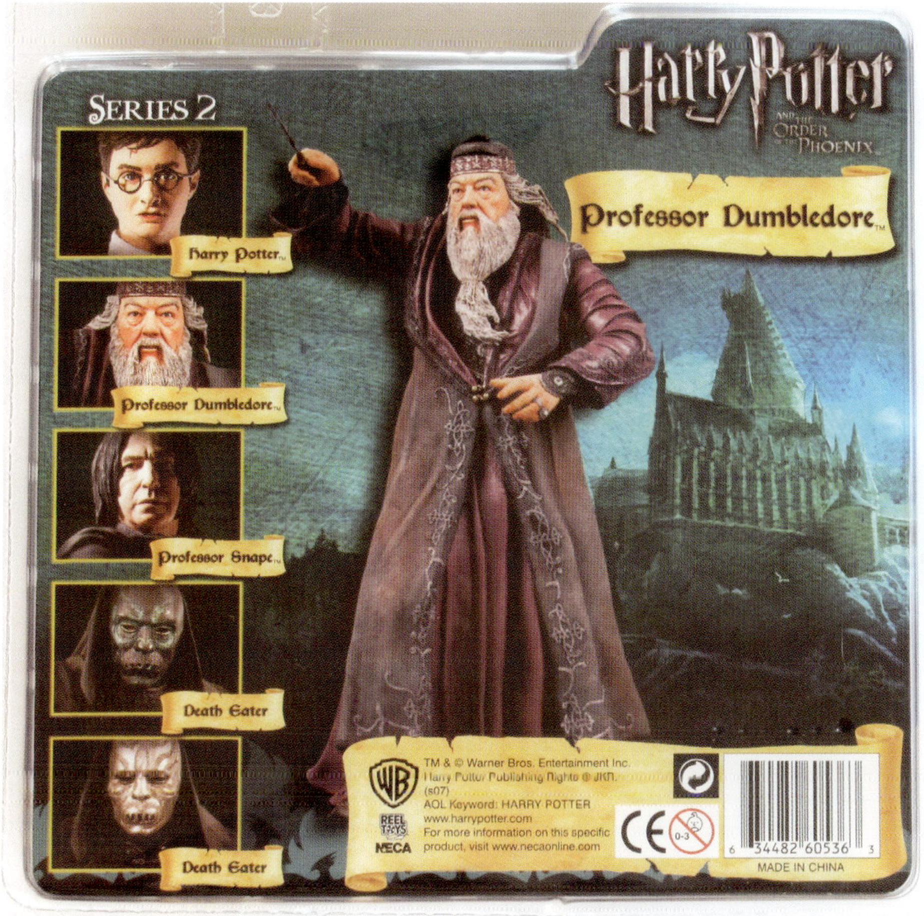
Harry Potter
and the Order of the Phoenix
Series 2
Harry Potter
Professor Dumbledore
Professor Snape
Death Eater
Death Eater
Professor Dumbledore
TM & © Warner Bros. Entertainment Inc.
Harry Potter Publishing Rights © JKR.
(s07)
AOL Keyword: HARRY POTTER
www.harrypotter.com
For more information on this specific product, visit www.necaonline.com
REEL TOYS
NECA
MADE IN CHINA

Harry Potter
and the Order of the Phoenix
Series 3
Bellatrix Lestrange
Harry Potter
Lucius Malfoy
Bellatrix Lestrange
TM & © Warner Bros. Entertainment Inc.
Harry Potter Publishing Rights © JKR.
(s07)
AOL Keyword: HARRY POTTER
www.harrypotter.com
For more information on this specific
product, visit www.necaonline.com
REEL TOYS
NECA
6 34482 49157 7
MADE IN CHINA

Series 1
Harry Potter
and the Order of the Phoenix
Sirius Black
Hermione Granger
Harry Potter
Ron Weasley
TM & © Warner Bros. Entertainment Inc.
Harry Potter Publishing Rights © JKR.
(s07)
AOL Keyword: HARRY POTTER
www.harrypotter.com
For more information on this specific
product, visit www.necaonline.com
NECA
MADE IN CHINA
NECA c/o Francis Melinek
Star Images
35 D Newington Green
London N16 9PR
UNITED KINGDOM
0-3

Harry Potter
Half-Blood Prince
Harry Potter
Ginny Weasley
Draco Malfoy
Mad-Eye Moody
Mad-Eye Moody & Draco Malfoy
Harry Potter & Ginny Weasley
TM & © Warner Bros. Entertainment Inc.
Harry Potter Publishing Rights © JKR.
(s09)
AOL Keyword: HARRY POTTER
www.harrypotter.com
For more information on this specific
product, visit www.necaonline.com
MADE IN CHINA

Series 1
Harry Potter
Half-Blood Prince
Draco Malfoy
Lord Voldemort
Ginny Weasley
Harry Potter
TM & © Warner Bros. Entertainment Inc.
Harry Potter Publishing Rights © JKR.
(s09)
AOL Keyword: HARRY POTTER
www.harrypotter.com
For more information on this specific
product, visit www.necaonline.com
MADE IN CHINA